NO
WAY

*for the
Spiritually
"Advanced"*

by
Ram Tzu

Illustrations by
Ted Kingdon

Advaita Press

Printed on acid-free paper

0 9 8 7 6 5 4 3 2

Copyright © 1990 by Advaita Press

First Published in United States Of America by:

Advaita Press
P.O. Box 3479
Redondo Beach, California 90277

Cover Illustration by: Richard Ewing

Cover design by: John McClung

Library of Congress Catalog Card No: 90-82091

ISBN 0-929448-13-8

NO
WAY

INTRODUCTION

I first met Ram Tzu in early 1990. He burst upon me, unexpected and unannounced, with a few of these verses. I was immediately captivated.

He looked fairly ordinary except for a distinct twinkle about the eyes and an odd, bemused smile. He told me he had been living in a place of his own construction in an unspecified locale for some time but beyond that he was totally unwilling to discuss anything of a personal nature.

He told me that he had no desire to become a *guru*, I think the exact phrase was, "I don't want a bunch of miserable seekers cluttering up my living room." When I pressed him as to why he had chosen me to look at his work (fishing for a compliment), he simply replied, "It seemed like a good idea at the time". He added that I was free to do with them as I pleased. His one condition was that his anonymity be maintained. This remains easy to do since I haven't a clue as to who he *really* is, where he came from or where he has gone.

Since that first meeting, I have been receiving occasional shipments of these little gems. They are always delivered by courier and always originate from a different place. I hope you find them as enlightening as I have.

They are presented here unedited.

Wayne Liquorman
Los Angeles, July 1990

1.

Ram Tzu has some questions for you...

Just who do you think you are?
Are you other than God?
Are you separate from Me?

If so....
What are you made of?
Where did it come from?

Don't look to science to help you.
The physicists have all become mystics.
They're of no more use to you than is Ram Tzu.

If you're really clever you'll turn around
And walk away
Fast!
Hang around here and you're liable to lose
Everything you hold dear.

Go back to your church, your temple,
Your therapist, your drug dealer, your *ashram*.
There you may find a moments peace.
You found it there once.
Here is only emptiness for you.
You'll find no food for your *ego* here.

What if your precious sense of self
Were to shrivel up and die?
Where would you be then?
What would happen?

Best not to risk it.

2.

Ram Tzu has a question for you...

You are kind to others.
You give to charity.
You go to church.
You pray with sincerity.
You are honest in your business.
You fulfill your obligations.
You know yourself to be a good man.

Where did these qualities come from?
How is it that your heart is not swollen
With the rage and despair
That causes a man
To slaughter his children?

Are you really so different from him?

Follow the spoor of your blessings
To their source.

There will be God.

3.

You can be seen sitting for hours
Palms turned to heaven
Eyes shut
Your breath even as it exits your nose.
Your attention is focused.
You've been doing this for awhile now
You're getting good at it.

At first you could barely sit five minutes
Now you can disappear for hours.

Ram Tzu has a question for you...

Why do you come back?

4.

You believe in affirmations.
You raise your voice to heaven
Proclaiming all you think you deserve.
Health, wealth, happiness
All yours for the asking.

You are careful not to appear greedy.
You ask for others also.

You can point with pride at
The obvious benefits of your faith.
Your lot has unquestionably improved.

Ram Tzu has a question for you...

Why did this simple procedure
Not occur to the man who just starved to death?

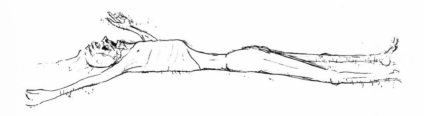

5.

Ram Tzu knows this...

It's a lie
It's all a lie.
The Buddha, Christ, Mohammed
Moses, Lao Tzu,
All were consummate liars.

Blasphemer explain yourself!

The Truth cannot be known
In the way you think of knowledge.
It does not make sense.
It functions in a realm
Closed to the mind.

The first utterance about Truth
Is the first step
Down the path of deceit.

In fact --

These very words are
But another turd
On the dung heap
Of what passes for Truth.

6.

Ram Tzu knows this...

The fear never leaves you.
It is part of you
As tied to your center as your breath.

Touch it,
Stroke it
Get to know it well.
As long as you are
It will be with you.

You scream
You shout
You rage
You want quit of it.
You push it away with all your strength.

But hear this...

It thrives on all this exercise
You give it.
It gets stronger when
You give it something to push against.

Left alone it will wither and die.

But you know you can not leave it alone.
You must always fight the fear.
It is your nature to always fight.

Yet sometimes there is Grace...
You disappear into it
And there is no longer a battle.

The warrior is gone.

7.

Ram Tzu knows this...

You will never have enough.
There is not enough to be had.

Your satisfaction,
However sweet,
Is always temporary.
And when it goes
It leaves behind a void
That screams to be filled.

So you go again in search
Of completeness,
Of fullness
Of peace,
Of happiness.
But you know only to look
For satisfaction.

A blind man in search of the sky.

You clever ones will see
It to be a problem with
A simple solution.

Austerity...

You strip yourself of worldly goods
Run about naked
Living off the labor of the crass souls
Still bound to the yoke of desire.

Pity it doesn't work.
It looks so good on paper.
But always in the deep,
Dark recesses of your soul
Lurks a tickle of noble want...

To be one with God.

It might just as well be a Rolls Royce.

Fools, don't despair.
For you there is always hope.

8.

Ram Tzu knows this...

All that ever was

Is

And forever will be.

9.

Ram Tzu knows this...

The more you pursue it
The further away it goes.

The harder you struggle
The deeper you sink.

Only a drunk can
Truly be sober.
Only a whore can
Truly be chaste.

Life is no place
For idle speculation.
No one has ever learned
From the mistakes of others.

A lie cloaked in truth
Is still a lie.
If it makes sense to you
You're in real trouble.

You always look for God
In high places...
Guess again.

Ram Tzu is not your friend
If you find him
Kill him.

10.

Ram Tzu knows this...

God doesn't care
What you had for lunch.
He created *tofu* and sausage
With the same thought.

Yet you advanced ones
Swell with pride
Convinced your special diet
Is a shortcut to heaven.

Clever you.
Who would have ever thought
To look *there*.

The fools go on eating poison
In blissful ignorance.
Too stupid and unspiritual
Not to enjoy their
Ice cream, french fries and red meat.

Ram Tzu says...

Far better to die a single death
Than a thousand little daily ones.

11.

Ram Tzu loves you...

So he is out to destroy you.

He knows you are your own
Worst enemy
So to destroy you
Is to save you.

Your ego must be smashed
Or you will surely die.
Yet words are like
Sledge hammers with greased handles.
They're difficult to guide
To their target,
Dangerous,
Liable to hit anything.

Ram Tzu loves you.
You can trust him.
Just put your head right here.
That's it.
Nothing to worry about...

Why do you hesitate?

12.

Ram Tzu knows you...

All of your
Dirty little secrets
Are tattooed on your forehead
For him to read.

You cling so tenaciously
To your history
Sensing correctly that to let go
Would set you adrift in a present
In which you cannot survive.

Here and now is the great evaporator
Poof...you're gone.
Surprising isn't it?
All that time you thought you were
You really weren't.

Poof...back again so soon?
Guess the illusion wasn't finished
With you after all.

If you learned anything
You'll know it doesn't
Make any difference.

Ram Tzu certainly doesn't care.

13.

You clever ones
Are beyond the reach
Of a paternal God.

You put your faith
In the esoteric
To protect it
From your cynicism.

Now you come
Sniffing around Ram Tzu
As if he were
A bitch in heat.

You hope to get
Your spiritual rocks off.

Ram Tzu knows this...

Your orgasm,
Your experience of God,
(Should you be lucky enough to have one)
Will not be Enlightenment,
But the result of masturbation.

14.

Ram Tzu is a madman...

He rants and raves
Spits, shouts
Waves his arms and
Talks gibberish.
All to get the attention
Of phantoms.

The authorities take
A dim view
Of such behavior--
Ask Jesus.

If Ram Tzu were clever
He would lay low.
No one likes
Their existence questioned--
It's disturbing.

If you don't like
Ram Tzu's ravings
Take heart...

His disciples will eventually
Render him palatable.

15.

Ram Tzu knows this...

You may obliterate your own body
But you will never kill your self.

When egos destroy their habitat
It is a monumental display of conceit,
An infant throwing all its toys
Out of its playpen,
Pitiful as the chest pounding
Of a gorilla in a zoo.

Who is fooled by your posturing?

You are powerless
Devoid of substance
As free to choose as
Characters in a play.

What makes you believe
In your own reality?

Find the answer to this
And meet God.

16.

You are a delver into
Your past lives.
You were once a queen,
Once a murderess, once a witch.
Never were you ordinary.
Never dull.
Never boring (until now).

Ram Tzu has a question for you...

What is reborn each time?
What is it made of?
Where does it come from?
Why do you love it so?

When you find out...
Come tell Ram Tzu.

Then he will have just
One more question for you.

17.

Ram Tzu knows this...

You can have everything
If you don't want more
Than you've got.

Unfortunately,
Not one of you
In the whole history
Of the world
Has ever been satisfied.

Pisses you off,
Doesn't it.

18.

Ram Tzu knows this...

You've never known
What's good for you.
Not really.

You've always chosen the way
Of least or greatest resistance.

The middle way,
The way without struggle,
Is frightening to you.

In the middle of the river
Where the current runs
Swift and deep
All your efforts
Are meaningless.

There you will surely drown.

That would be terrible.

19.

Ram Tzu knows this...

Your very best thinking
Got you into this mess.

What obstructs
Your view of the truth
Is all that you know,
All that you hold sacred.

If you wish to truly
See the sunlight
Dance on the leaves
You must have
Clean windows.

Ram Tzu asks...

Who does windows?

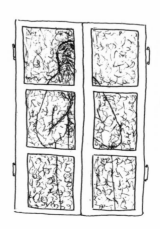

20.

Ram Tzu knows this...

You are caught
In a web of beliefs.
You spin them from
Your own abdomen.
They are made from
The substance of your self.

You believe in
Your own power.

You consider yourself
The Source.
Even though
When under duress
You pay lip service
To an all powerful God.

You believe in
The supremacy of technique.

You are convinced that if
You can but manage...

Your mind
Your money
Your time

Your breath
Your energy
Your body
Your faith
Your relationships
Your prayers

You will unlock the door
To happiness, peace and contentment.

Guess again.

21.

Ram Tzu will be misunderstood
On many levels...

You clever ones
Will grasp his meaning immediately.

You fools
Will think it all bullshit.

You scholars
Will draw parallels.

You clerics
Will reframe it to fit your dogma.

You pious ones
Will be shocked.

You sinners
Will be too busy to care.

A very few of you
Won't give it a moments thought.

But all of you
Are secretly delighted
That someone is paying you
Even the slightest attention.

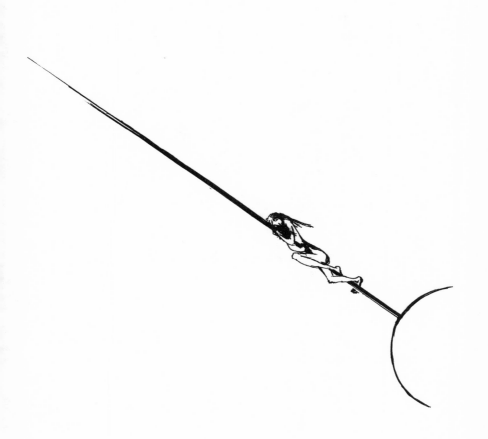

22.

Your New Age
Is neither new
Nor will it last an age.

You ride a pendulum
On a clock wound
To run for eternity.

Your despair has
Today turned to hope.
Tomorrow it will
Turn back again.

The walls of oppression
You tear down here
Will be rebuilt
There.

The meek shall
Inherit the earth
Then the clever ones
Will take it back from them.

The torture chamber
Will empty
And refill.

A disease will
Be conquered
And a new one will
Appear to takes its place.

This strikes you
As a bleak vision
But Ram Tzu knows this...

It is your hope for a better future
That keeps you in chains today.

23.

Ram Tzu knows this...

You clever ones
Are always looking for a way
To beat the system.

You want Enlightenment
You want eternal bliss
You want the ultimate orgasm
You want it all...
And
You want to be around
To enjoy it.

This renders you
The ultimate sucker.
You are fair game.

You get baptized and analyzed.
You get rolfed and ESTed.
You meditate and vegetate.
You're rebirthed and realigned.
You're fucked and sucked.
You chant, you rant,
You heal the child within.
You collect money in airports.
You get in touch with your feelings.
You have your palms, your cards,
Your auras and your chakras read.

If you're very clever
You go to India, Tibet,
Thailand, China...

In your heart
You know the Truth is incompatible
With indoor plumbing.

You humbly contract dysentery or hepatitis.
You pretend that Sai Baba
Is different from Oral Roberts.

It's a wonder Ram Tzu hasn't died laughing.

24.

Ram Tzu has not come
To mock you.
Ram Tzu has not come
To blame you.
Ram Tzu is here merely
To destroy you.

He couldn't care less
What you think.
He doesn't want
Your sex
Your money
Your reverence.

He has no interest
In your precious soul.
He'll leave the battle for that
To others.

Ram Tzu has but a single task for you...

Try to imagine
An act
Without motivation.

Did you try it?

Leaves you wondering
Just who's in charge here,
Doesn't it?

25.

Ram Tzu knows this...

There is less here
Than meets the eye.

26.

Ram Tzu knows this...

It's not your fault.
How could it be?

A shadow is not responsible
For its movements.

A knife cannot
Be tried for murder.

You have been filled
With your self.

You believe what
You are meant to believe.

You go where
You are supposed to go.

Ram Tzu does not offer advice...

Who would he offer it to?

27.

Most of what
You call love
Is just business.

You demand
Sufficient return
On your investment
Or you go elsewhere.

No one likes to
Suffer a loss.

After all,
If you don't manage
Your portfolio
Who will?

It's not the sort of thing
You want to leave to chance.

Problem is
You're always in fear
You're always hedging.

Ram Tzu knows this...

It's a losing proposition
Trying to keep that
Which you haven't got.

28.

Ram Tzu knows this...

Eastern mystical bullshit

And

Western mystical bullshit
Have a common denominator.

Need he state
The scatologically obvious?

The Truth
Is buried in the Eastern dung heap.
A few will find it there.

Others will make the discovery
In the Western sewer,
Where the Truth was
Flushed centuries ago.

You are shocked to find
God linked to shit
Rather than sunsets and puppies.

It disturbs you to
Think of Him
Wielding a knife
In an abattoir.

Ram Tzu sees God everywhere...

Even in you.

29.

Ram Tzu knows this...

You won't get out of this alive.

30.

Ram Tzu knows this...

When a glimmer of
Understanding appears,
You have cancer.

It will grow...
Relentlessly replacing
You with Itself.

Until you are gone.

31.

You are cursed
With a belief in the
Appropriate.

You are enslaved
By your belief
In your
Self.

Like a dog
On the freeway,
Your options
Are limited,
Unappealing.

Small wonder
You're a little
Nervous.

Small wonder
You seek
A way
Out.

If Ram Tzu believed in you...

You would have his sympathies.

32.

Ram Tzu knows this...

There is a hole
Inside you that
You try desperately
To fill up.

You pour in
Various satisfactions
To make yourself
Feel alright.

Sometimes,
If you can get enough,
The hole fills to the brim
And there is a
Blissful moment of evenness.

But your hole is open
At the bottom.
It's contents always leak through
Leaving you empty
Again
And desperate
For more.

Ram Tzu knows what must be done...

You must be thrown in the hole.

33.

You move mindfully
Towards tenderness.
You jump mindlessly
Away from the whip.

Ram Tzu loves you
So he whips you.

Ram Tzu knows this...

That last step off the cliff
Is always a surprise.

34.

Ram Tzu believes
In the law
Of cause and effect.

He just doesn't know
Which is which.

35.

You want consistency
You want security
You want to maintain
The illusion
Of being in control.

It's hard to manage
When things keep changing.
You have to be
Constantly on guard.

But change is inescapable,
It's a symptom of time,
It's built into the system.

Ask your physicist

Without change
The Universe collapses.

Ram Tzu has a question for you...

Why do you keep on
Spitting into the wind?

36.

Ram Tzu knows this...

You are willing
To take limitless blame,
So long as you
Can keep getting
A little credit.

37.

Ram Tzu hears it all the time...

You had a profound, revealing,
Deeply moving spiritual experience.
Now you're hooked.
Now you want more.
Now you're a seeker.

No junkie has ever
Been more dedicated
Or more continually disappointed
Or more miserable.

Once you might
Have been satisfied
With a new car
Or a loving mate.

Now you will settle
For nothing less
Than union with God.

Ram Tzu knows this...

You're fucked.

38.

You believe in yourself.
You believe in
The power of positive thinking.
You attend seminars
To gain control of your life.

Once again you become pregnant
With visions of limitless opportunities,
All yours for the grabbing.

You need merely to
Set your goals
Define your wants
Establish priorities.

Then you can march off
To claim all
That is rightfully yours.

Ram Tzu has a question for you...

What went wrong this time?

39.

Ram Tzu knows this...

You are perfect.

Your every defect
Is perfectly defined.

Your every blemish
Is perfectly placed.

Your every absurd action
Is perfectly timed.

Only God could make
Something this ridiculous

Work.

40.

You cry for
Sympathy and kindness
Tolerance and understanding.

All Ram Tzu gives you
Are more insults
And cruel insinuations
About your origin (or lack thereof).

You point to the Biggies,
Jesus, Krishna, Buddha,
All gentleness and compassion.
You demand he be more like them.

Ram Tzu has some questions for you...

Where are these guys
Now that you need them?

And

Why did they leave you here
With the likes of Ram Tzu?

41.

You promise you'll change
You swear you'll do better
And maybe you will.

Ram Tzu knows this...

It won't be by your own power.

42.

You clever ones
Are wise to
Ram Tzu's game.
You won't be taken in
By such sophistry.

You devout ones
Simply dismiss him
As the devils tool.

You blessed ones
Couldn't care less
What Ram Tzu knows.

You fools look right through him
As if he wasn't there.

43.

Many of you
Are long time seekers and scholars.
You are well versed
In Eastern Mystical Bullshit.

You have learned
From *vedas* and *sutras*
That it's all just a dream
You dream while awake.

Ram Tzu has a question for you...

What makes you think
You are the dreamer
Not the dreamed?

44.

Ram Tzu knows this...

You indulge in
Self improvement

And

All you have to show for it
Is an improved self.

45.

Ram Tzu knows this...

The Truth is unspeakable.
It can only be pointed at.

The more elaborate and ornate
The sign post
The more easily do you
Mistake it for the destination.

Except for you
Oh so spiritual ascetics.

For you...

The plainer and simpler
The sign post
The more easily do you
Mistake it for the destination.

46.

You have experienced
Being in the flow.
You have known moments
Of profound effortlessness.

The golf club seemed to swing itself.
The poem leapt onto the page.
The exact right word flew from your lips.
The solution to the problem just *appeared*.

In these moments
There was no doubt.
All questions vanished.
Time changed shape or evaporated.
You disappeared.

But always
Your ego reasserted itself
And claimed the experience
As its own.

Believing you had done something
You set out to do it again.
You developed techniques, therapies, religions.

Ram Tzu has a question for you?

What force makes you believe
You can manufacture Grace?

47.

Ram Tzu knows this...

You respond to flattery.

You adore being
Told that you are:

Pure Love
Ultimate Goodness
Perfection
God
Everything Wonderful and Worthwhile

You flock to Masters
That reassure you
You're not the debased
Little asshole
You secretly know yourself to be.

Guess what?

The You they are talking about
Isn't you.

48.

Ram Tzu knows this...

Nothing is unexplainable.

Everything is a mystery.

49.

First...

You use your mind as
The ultimate jigsaw.
You take Totality
And cut it up
Into a million tiny pieces.

Then...

Having tired of that game,
You sit down and try to
Reassemble this jumble of pieces
Into something comprehensible.

Ram Tzu knows...

God invented time
Just so you could do this.

50.

You're a MileagePlus seeker...

You go to Bali
To eat purple mushrooms
That grow out of sacred cow shit.

You go to Mexico
To eat cactus buttons
With ancient medicine men.

You go to the Amazon
To snort tree bark
With the primitives.

You go to Africa
To smoke spiritual weed
With witch-doctors.

You cavort with spirits
You see God
You become One with the Universe.

Ram Tzu has a question for you...

Why do you keep buying
Round trip tickets?

51.

You clever ones
Have learned that:

All effort is useless...
Nothing is left to chance...
God is running the show...
You are but a robot.

Ram Tzu has a question for you...

What makes you keep trying?

52.

You clever ones
Go looking
For a Master
In a cave
In the Himalayas
Or in the forests
Of Thailand.

If you're less clever
You'll look for him
Somewhere comfortable
Like Ashland, Sedona,
Santa Fe or Santa Cruz.

Wouldn't you be surprised
To learn that
All this time
He was sitting behind a desk
In your bank?

Ram Tzu knows this...

You require your sages
To be in proper uniform.

53.

Ram Tzu knows this...

If you had a choice
You would *never*
Let go of the illusion.

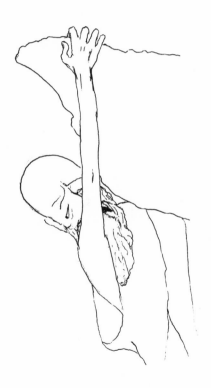

54.

All you really wanted
Was enough.

Which is to say
You only wanted more.

Ram Tzu knows this...

What you now have
Is all you'll *ever* have.

55.

You clothe your
Most sacred illusions
In finery of
Piety, purity and reverence.

You view them only by candlelight
And burn clouds of incense to
Obscure all the blood, shit and sperm.

You enforce strict solemnity
Knowing that
If the laughter got started
It would never stop.

Ram Tzu knows why
It is called Illumination.

56.

You stand at the edge
Ready to throw yourself in.

What a shock to discover

There is no where to go
And no one to throw.

57.

If you are happy
Run away from Ram Tzu.

Ram Tzu's venom is only safe
If you're already snake-bit.

58.

Your Master told you...

The Way is to *be*,
Without questions.

Now you want to know,
How do you do that?

59.

Ram Tzu has a question for you...

If you don't define yourself
By what others think of you.

And

You don't define yourself
By what you think of you.

What are you?

60.

Give it up!
Forget it!
You're never going
To be Enlightened.

Don't bother trying.
All effort is useless.
You don't stand a chance.
Why struggle?

You work hard at it
And you only end up
Fodder for the priests
And other hucksters.

Don't let them con you.
No one in the whole
History of man
Has ever made it.

Ram Tzu knows this...

You are not going to be

The first.

61.

Ram Tzu knows this...

Hoping and worrying
Keep you occupied
While you're waiting
For something to happen.

62.

You complain to Ram Tzu...

You're tired of mysticism.
You're sick of paradox.
You want to know what's going on.

If you want meaning
Take these words to
Your professor
Or your priest.

It is their job
To make something
Out of nothing.

63.

Ram Tzu knows this...

You can only be lost
If you are trying
To get somewhere.

64.

You believe in free will.
You believe you make yourself sick.
You believe you choose your own parents.
You believe you can control your dreams.
You believe you can take charge of your life.
You believe there is a child within that you can heal.
You believe you have the power of prayer.
You believe that you can make a difference.
You believe your pain is your fault.
You believe you can do better.
You believe you are responsible
You believe all sorts of shit.

Ram Tzu knows this...

When God wants you to do something
You believe it's your own idea

65.

Ram Tzu knows this...

For every harmony
There is a chaos.

For every order
There is a disorder.

Back and forth
Up and down
Yin and Yang.

All attempts at stasis
Are doomed,
Crushed under
The relentless wheel
Of nature.

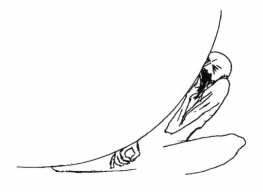

66.

Ram Tzu knows this...

Every time
You find an answer,
The question
No longer seems important.

67.

You demand to know...

How can Ram Tzu laugh
As you are being tortured?

Can't he see you
Being stretched
On a rack
Of your own thoughts?

Can't he see
Your pain
As your ego
Relentlessly turns the wheel?

Ram Tzu sees...

You clutch the ropes
That appear to bind you.
There are no knots.
Nothing else holds you down.

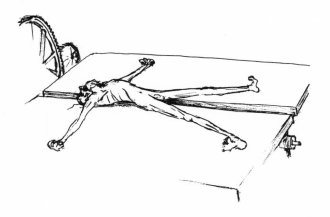

68.

Ram Tzu knows this...

Only a fool
Would trade
Everything he has

For nothing.

69.

Ram Tzu knows this...

A few of you very clever ones
Have figured out
The metaphysical puzzle
And boy are you ever proud.

You condescendingly watch
The fools flounder about
Their wretched little lives
Ignorant of the Truth
As you know it.

Meanwhile
You grow increasingly isolated.
You sit cold and aloof
In your lofty domain.

Until
One day you realize
You're old
And alone
And afraid

And oh so very clever.

70.

Ram Tzu was born in silence
And undoubtedly will return there.

For the present
His task is
To scream, spit
Bite, scratch,
Hoot, holler
And generally
Make a nuisance of himself.

This will last
Until it's over.

71.

What could be more ludicrous
Or more boring
Than a discussion about the Truth?

The same bullshit keeps being repeated
Over and over and over
Generation after generation
Century upon century.

The rabbis keep crowing about
Their chosen status.

The mullahs keep sending
Their faithful off to holy slaughter.

The priests and nuns keep stewing
In their own sexual juices.

The atheists keep worshiping
Their god of reason.

All have their texts of support
All have their rationale.

Ram Tzu knows this...

No one
In the whole history of the argument
Has ever been right.

72.

You want your purveyors of Truth
To look and act special.

You want them different
And separate
And powerful.

You prefer to imagine them
Cloaked in light
Than sitting on the toilet.

You like them passionless, sexless,
Mellow, gentle and kind.

You like the idea of miracles
And will invent them when necessary.

Your strategy is to keep them
Out there
Far away from you
Exotic and mysterious.

You revel in the myth
Of the Enlightened individual
Hoping to someday be so empowered.

What you can't tolerate
Is for them to appear
As ordinary as you.

Ram Tzu knows this...

You always miss the Truth
Because it is too plain to see.

73.

The priests
Hound you with orders
You know
You don't have the power
To carry out.

This leaves you
Feeling guilty
And inadequate.

Ram Tzu knows this...

They've got you
Right where they want you.

74.

Once the questions start
They quickly gather momentum.

The more you know
The more you need to know.

Ram Tzu realizes...

Having all the answers
Means transcending all the questions.

75.

You read the
Spiritual guidebooks.
God on $25 a Day.

You are inspired.
You can't wait to see
All the sights
So eloquently described.

It all sounds
Much more exciting
Than what you have at home.

But the fear sets in
When it's time to leave.
You try to pack
Everything you own.

Now you can't move
For the weight of it.

Ram Tzu knows this...

If you finally go
You'll travel *light.*

76.

Ram Tzu knows this...

You think
Ram Tzu is talking
About someone else.

77.

You look for clues.
You search for the key
That will unlock the mystery.

You gaze into the entrails of chickens
You map the movements of the stars
You count your breaths
You chant your pet name for God
You consult cards
You add up numbers
You have endless sex
You fast
You take drugs
You study scripture
You read tea leaves
You talk to spirits
You twist your body into fascinating shapes
You guru hop
You attend seminars and retreats
You exercise
You buy books
You listen to tapes
You pray with all your might

Ram Tzu knows this...

When you are done with these
There you are.

78.

You hold on to your life
With the same passion
That you cling to your money
And your mate.

Once you feared death
More than any other loss
It seemed so permanent.

Then one of you
Very clever ones
Invented reincarnation
And made death seem temporary.

Ram Tzu knows this...

The door to immortality
Is always right here
And it is forever locked to you.

79.

You think something's wrong
There must have been a mistake

You think things should be different
By different you mean better
And you're pretty sure
You know what better is.

You would eliminate
All the "bad" stuff:

War
Disease
Suffering
Famine
Pollution

Would be good for starters.

Who could argue with that?

You would save cute animals
You would ban bombs
You would halt injustice
You would make everyone happy.

Why not?
It could happen.

And if it does, Ram Tzu knows this...

God will be grateful
For your help.

80.

In Ram Tzu's world:

Nothing is sacred.
Consistency is a thing
Of the past.
Reason is unreasonable.
The sun shines at night.
Children raise their parents.
Ugliness is beautiful.
Fools are respected.
Dreams are dreamed while awake.
Old men are born.
The ordinary is special.
There are no mistakes.

In Ram Tzu's world:

Nothing remains undone
And
No one ever does anything.

81.

None of you
Are comfortable
With paradox.

You see it
As a blight
On the
Intellectual landscape.

It's unmanageable.
It can't be contained.
It slithers out of your grasp.
It oozes through your fingers.
It pisses you off.

Ram Tzu knows this...

In your world dependent on opposites
There can be no unity.

82.

You murder
Then eat
Plants
Instead of animals.

You believe that this
Brings you closer to God.

It's a petty virtue
But it makes you proud
To be so pure
And so spiritual.

Ram Tzu knows this...

You are not what you eat
You are what God thinks.

83.

You believe in creative visualization
But you can only extrapolate
From what you have already seen.

You can't visualize Peace
Only the absence of turmoil.

You can't visualize Wholeness
Only the absence of fragmentation.

You can't visualize Harmony
Only the absence of discord.

You can't visualize Love
Only the absence of hate.

You can't visualize Joy
Only the absence of sorrow.

Ram Tzu knows this...

There can be Peace,
Wholeness, Harmony,
Love, Joy.

But not if you're there.

84.

Ram Tzu knows this...

Your life is a journey
In which
No one is going any where.

85.

You think of the Path
As a long arduous climb
Up the mountain.

You concede there may be
Many paths
But you're sure
All have the same
Exalted goal.

Ram Tzu knows this...

There are many Paths.

Like streams
They flow effortlessly
(though not necessarily painlessly)
Down the mountain.

All disappear
Into the desert sands below.

86.

Ram Tzu knows this...

Nothing can be said

So

There's always
More to say.

87.

You disdain political power
You're too ethereal for that.

You scorn economic power
You're to egalitarian for that.

You abhor military power
You're to peaceful for that.

You like *chi* power,
Kundalini power,
Prayer power,
The power of positive thinking.

You think there is a difference.

Ram Tzu knows this...

Egos need fuel.

88.

Ram Tzu knows this...

You have tasted ecstasy
Drunk deeply of its nectar.

So you embrace it
Or reject it.

What does it matter?

Addict or ascetic
You are caught in the web
Of your own ego.

The harder you struggle
The more surely
You call the spider.

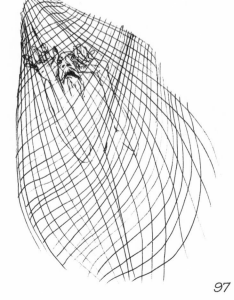

89.

You have
The cold, clear stare
Of the righteous.

You're skilled.
You're competent.
You're calm.
You're clean.
You're flawless.
Your mother says you're brilliant.

You have the answers.
You know what's up.
You're independent.
You're free of attachment.

You consider yourself
A winner.

Ram Tzu knows this...

You'll play until
Things get messy.

You don't like mess.

90.

Ram Tzu knows this...

You seek ascendence
Where there is only transcendence.

Yet there is hope.

You may be so busy
Looking at the heavens
You'll stumble over the edge.

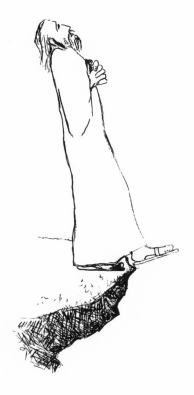

91.

What you call spirituality
Is nothing more
Than a collection
Of management techniques.

You search for methods
To cope with problems
You don't even have yet.

You seek ways to escape
A reality
You are never in.

Ram Tzu knows this...

Whoever said:

"There is no time like the present."

Was right.

92.

Search for Truth
If you must.
But don't forget
To take out the garbage..

93.

You like the idea of
Being on a journey.

You like the idea
That you're going somewhere.

You think
If you're going somewhere
You might get somewhere.

You're seduced by
The prospect of progress.

It's a measure of your discontent.

Ram Tzu knows this...

You can't get here
From there.

94.

Ram Tzu hears you...

You're getting sick of this.
You demand to know
Who's in charge?
Who's responsible for this mess?

You want answers
And you want them *now*.

And while you're at it
You demand to know
Who's this "you"
That Ram Tzu is talking to?

It's all just too confusing.

You're beginning to suspect
Ram Tzu has been
Less than forthright.

95.

Ram Tzu knows this...

If you looked in the mirror
And saw no reflection of yourself
You would naturally assume
There was something wrong
With the mirror.

So it is
You suspect
There is
Something wrong
With Ram Tzu.

96.

You want out
You want escape
You want relief.

You meditate
To block out life.
You chant
To put the world on hold.
You pray
To get what you want.
You take drugs
To get there faster.

Ram Tzu knows this...

Your noble search for God
Is but a sly dodge.

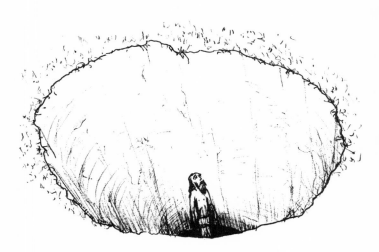

97.

You have Ram Tzu's love
And you've done nothing
To deserve it.

Now you want
Ram Tzu's approval.

You've run out of luck.